Cipota under the

MOON

Cipota under the

MOON

poems

Claudia Castro Luna

TIA CHUCHA PRESS

Book Design: Jane Brunette

Cover Art: from the Museo Nacional de Antropología Dr. David J. Guzmán, El Salvador (MUNA);
Antonio Bonilla, Muralist; Fred Ramos, Photograph Credit. Used with permission.

PUBLISHED BY:
Tía Chucha Press
A project of Tía Chucha's Centro Cultural, Inc.
PO Box 328
San Fernando, CA 91341
www.tiachucha.org

DISTRIBUTED BY:
Northwestern University Press
Chicago Distribution Center
11030 South Langley Avenue
Chicago IL 60628

Tía Chucha's Centro Cultural & Bookstore is a 501 (c) (3) nonprofit corporation funded in part over
the years by the Arts for Justice Fund, National Endowment for the Arts, California Arts Council, Los
Angeles County Arts Commission, Los Angeles Department of Cultural Affairs, The California Com-
munity Foundation, the Annenberg Foundation, the Weingart Foundation, the Lia Fund, National As-
sociation of Latino Arts and Culture, Ford Foundation, MetLife, Southwest Airlines, the Andy Warhol
Foundation for the Visual Arts, the Thrill Hill Foundation, the Middleton Foundation, Center for Cul-
tural Innovation, John Irvine Foundation, Not Just Us Foundation, Liberty Hill Foundation, the Attias
Family Foundation, and the Guacamole Fund, among others. Donations have also come from Bruce
Springsteen, John Densmore of The Doors, Jackson Browne, Lou Adler, Richard Foos, Gary Stewart,
Charles Wright, Adrienne Rich, Tom Hayden, Dave Marsh, Jack Kornfield, Jesus Trevino, David San-
doval, Gary Soto, Sandra Cisneros, Denise Chávez and John Randall of the Border Book Festival, Luis
& Trini Rodríguez, and others.

Contents

Sometimes You Are Permitted a Return

Aquí Nada Más

Para mi abuela, Carmen Vargas (Q.E.P.D.),
para mi hermana, Carmen Aída,
y para las cipotas y cipotes de El Salvador.

For my grandmother Carmen Vargas (R.I.P.),
for my sister Carmen Aída,
and for the girls and boys of El Salvador.

1

Notes from a
Home Country

Río Sucio

I dreamt of a dirty river
I dreamt of a white horse
the river didn't want a bridge on its back
the horse wanted to sleep on my lap

Agua de Beber

Once there was a girl who lived in a country called Fear. There
 her fingers cracked and split into sharp mouths that screamed
what she could not scream. Sometimes her hands itched, and she
scratched them viciously. With the scratching, her pores swelled.
At peak moments they burst, releasing the liquid within. The girl
feared many things but death most of all, not her own, but that
of her parents, through whom she saw and valued the world. That
little girl is still around: she lives inside me, sneaking pistachio ice
cream whenever she can. Now, when my hands begin to crack and
split, I panic and recoil from the pain this causes and from the
pain they caused the girl. Long ago my hands learned to cry in my
stead. They carved deltas at the tips of my fingers that took me
to ocean—Oh, how deep, how vast the great water, how it sloshes
inside my belly. Oh, how beautiful the world to which I belong.

Vía Láctea

Te dejo aquí, bajo la sombra de este mango. I leave you here, in the shade of this mango tree. Como quien dice esperando un bus en una esquina, o a la orilla de un río. Hablo de una vía que arrastra almas buenas y malas y cosas chulas y rotas. Imagine you are at a bus stop or standing on a riverbank, watching creatures and their beating hearts ambling by, counting the ways their faces flare up to both sides of the moon. Te dejo con un par de maracas pa'que acompañés a los muertos en su procesión y para que animés a los vivos en sus duelos. You are not alone. I am with you, here, naked, holding my baby teeth in a plastic bag, my back against the tree's rough bark, so that I may, alongside you, learn from it how to grow a spine. Ten cuidado con gatos maleantes, no te metás con doncellas traidoras listas para ofrecerte algún bocado. Fijate que estoy aquí contigo y desnuda. Bésame. Bésame mucho. Como te beso yo a tí. Kiss me. Kiss me deeply, like the earth embraces a tree's roots, like new lovers do when night falls.

El Salvador 1980

Violence spread like tincture inside a water glass. Like language it moved over, under, around, inside us. It trespassed membranes swiftly, like love and hate; it blistered our cells and soldered our joints. And when the blood of its cruelty spilled raw and irascible down the street and yonder, among the volcano's blue skirts, and in the crotch of a mountain gully, even water, the rivers that gave us life, could not launder away the ache.

Syndrome

You and your sister stand at a bus stop with a group of strangers
when a truck full of soldiers drives past, all of them holding
M-16s, all of them ready to kill on command. You and everyone
else know that if one person moves the wrong way, everyone goes.
It has happened before. You wait for the unleashed bullets, wait
for them to tear your flesh, wait for the cry of help that is already
seeping from your lips, wait for your last breath. This time the
convoy goes on past, and you and your little sister, in your check-
ered school skirts, squeeze onto the next bus that comes along.
On the ride home the city loses power. Armed forces versus
guerillas. Handguns versus assault rifles. Conviction versus orders.
You arrive home in darkness, your parents, half ghosts, waiting
at the front door. You are alive, but something inside you died
back at the bus stop. Your body has no way of metabolizing that
kind of fright. It swallows it instead, a barbed lump. Years later
a therapist gives it a name. By then the lump has burned, has
grown, is a parasite making rancid what once was whole.

Shade Grown

He belonged to those whose rank insignias, in addition to coronel, general, and sargento, indicated something about the state of their souls. Even children like me knew these men traded in cruelty, in the ways of torture and murder, in inflicting pain. In fatigues and with his eyes disappeared behind aviator sunglasses, his swagger gave off a kind of foul bloom. His was the only house in the colonia secured by a metal fence, and we knew he had a finca where he grew shade-grown coffee. Bodies were sometimes found at the edges of remote fincas, or along their twisty mountain roads. Whenever he visited his finca he returned with oranges piled in the bed of his pickup. The fruits were small and blotchy, like sickly suns orbiting his tenebrous universe, and he sold them in burlap sacks. We bought them, sliced them, squeezed them for every drop of juice that could be had. No one ever asked the fruits what cries of mercy they might have heard up in the cerros where clouds hang like hammocks over lush tree canopies. No one asked them about the sulphur reek of his step or about the coffee ripening beneath their branches. In clean glasses we drank their juice in thirsty gulps and at night asked the stars to keep and preserve us.

In the Vault of Your Hands

Memories gain parity
with longing
longing ossifies yearning
yearning taints the imagination
over time
what remains
is not the memory
but our desire of it
then again
some events return
years and years later
with the hum and spunk
of a lightning bolt
still throbbing
in the ejaculate
of the present tense

Vamos a la Escuela

We walked to school clean as clouds in our starched, white uniforms. Through the campus of the National University, the shortcut took us past buildings tagged with revolutionary slogans, banners draped over gun-shattered windows, walls pockmarked with bullet holes. These daily walks were instructive. Desecrated buildings served double-time as lesson and chalkboard. Our vocabulary expanded—

    ametrallado   quebrado

    baliado   tiroteado

    balaceado   pistoleado   acribillado

—as we learned that there was more than one way to say *riddled with bullets*. People died that way.

Garrison

Two girls slinked alongside barb-wired brick walls on their way
to swimming lessons, doing their best to remain collected past the
turrets stationed with armed soldiers. Ensconced in their look-
outs, the troopers held their metralletas close to their bodies, as
if they loved them, but not so much they would not use them ill.
After our lesson, we headed home the same way we walked to
the pool, guillotining chatter and laughter, scurrying along the
garrison's walls. Only the sound of our flip-flops striking our heels
betrayed us. What if today's soldiers were in a foul mood and
pulled their triggers? What if they noticed our bulging bags, our
weekly comings and goings, and tagged us as informants? What if,
right leg, what if, left leg, we got through it that way—like prayers
in a rosary—one bead, one foot in front of the other, one bead,
one foot, one bead, one foot all the way home.

Tyranny of the Milky Way

The way clouds taste as they go from castles to rabbits above your head. You are twelve, your skin damp from the humid tropical day, the grass under your arms and legs benign even if itchy. The way a million stars scatter at night, and you in jersey gown and bare feet seek the same spot from earlier in the day to count far away incandescent rocks. Tucked behind your ear your secret wish to spot a single UFO. The way a slice of tres leches cake on your thirteenth birthday surrenders in unison on your tongue its sweet milks. The way at twelve you tasted marvel and by fourteen you'd tasted war.

Hija de los Días

My fourteenth birthday happened in a November lost to a brackish year. Newspaper headlines from the first sixteen days of that month listed the following: on the second day ten bodies of unidentified young men were found ditched on the road to Apulo. Two days later a man was gunned down and killed in his car in northern San Salvador. The following day another man succumbed when his furniture store was attacked. On the seventh, in the city of Santa Ana, a thirteen-year-old boy and four adults were attacked and killed. On the fifteenth a union leader died of gunshot wounds. The next day a colonel, his wife, and his children, eleven and fifteen, were carbonized when incendiary bombs exploded in their house. Pecked days and plucked of hope. My parents did not sing my birthday. They must have felt war's vertigo, the gathering of ashes inside people and things. These days I pull weeds in my garden and just as soon new ones leaf back up. Is that resilience? Happy birthday, papá. Happy birthday, mamá. Happy birthday, happy birthday, happy birthday to you.

This Is Not a Poem

Guerra doesn't go away when the bullets stop, when the grenades
go silent, when helicopters' blades no longer kick up the dust of
innocents or presidential lies. There is no periphery to guerra.
I'll say, a giant cloaca, propelling its stench on the ground, in the
sky, under water, subcutaneously, clouding dreams, clogging guts,
silencing tongues. Guerra does not know of lazy Sunday mornings
or afternoon coffee breaks. It knows fear and death. I highly don't
recommend it.

Dios Madre

Behind the counter
tending to a customer
he could see her
skipping and laughing
in the middle of the street
children playing
under the midday sun
soon she would come in
for her almuerzo
then head back out to school

He bent his head
to count out change
that is when
it happened
that is when
bullets ripped
his world in defense
of nothing that matters

In a split second
children, dogs, birds
the ghosts
who live in trees
even the gunman
dispersed
—but she did not

She'd fallen
under the old almedra tree
and for a second
nothing glittered
nothing
not even the sun

He was too late
to her side. She, still
warm to the touch
her long hair wet
with her own blood

Bring a healer!
he screamed
a priest, a doctor, a witch!
hire a mountain
hire a god, hire two
he begged
someone, please, conjure a miracle!
sugar cane horizons trembled
and the looming volcano stirred

Cupped in his hands
his ten-year-old daughter
in her school uniform
passed from smiling
to hardened concrete

When she was under
nine days of prayers
and safely underground

he fled north
shoeless like rain

Somewhere along the road
he cut his head off
to scream less
he carried
cabeza and grief
under his arm for miles
then joined
a crowded bus
crossed a river
sat on the roof of a wagon train
crawled across a desert
his head facing upward
strapped to his back
better not to see her
in every girl he came across

He now lives in a place
where people see him as he is not
call him names not his own
illegal they say
among other things
the man he was is no longer
but he is still a father
her father

Somedays in the hustle
to find food and shelter
a second passes and he doesn't
doesn't think of her

For Alfredo Espino

If I had wings
this morning!
If I had wings
soar to the blue
with frank scissors
cut enough sky
fashion a cape
place it on my shoulders
become a kind of shero
who speaks
with the eloquence of wind
the fairness of light
the truth of children's eyes
to excise once and for all
the muck soiling
men's hearts

Caravans

Marching to the tune of millions of dollars in military aid, a caravan set out in 1980 from the United States toward El Salvador. As part of it, more than 32,000 M16A1/A2 rifles snaked southward, each machine capable of dislodging 800 rounds of ammunition per minute—800 bullets per minute on the first day, the second, and every subsequent day for twelve years. Years of dispatching obedient bullets to seek and kill the soft bodies that were their targets. Three decades and thousands of deaths later, a new caravan, not of weapons but of war survivors, inches north to the place where the rifles came from. Women pushing strollers, fathers and sons, fathers and daughters, walking hundreds of miles, walking. A boy walks wearing a scapular, the cloth soaked with holy water now encrusted with sweat. A woman walks carrying fresh fear in her belly. The inevitability of their steps over their silent unforgetting. On the way, an angry river drowns the voices of a young father and his toddler daughter. The two, face down, her little arm around his neck.

The shortest distance between two points is a straight line. Sometimes the line in question bends on itself, takes a rapacious detour, orbits around the sun a few times. So it is that yesterday's bullets claim bodies today.

Angelitos

Of all humans, dead children alone possess the innocence
and grace to be granted unquestioned and immediate entry into
Heaven. Their bodies, tenderly clothed in milk and lace, are laid
to rest in white coffins lined in pearly satin. Whenever possible,
ruffles of white crêpe paper adorn the outside of their funeral
boxes. Whenever possible, a circlet of ivory flowers crowns the
girls. Sometimes a white band with a paper cross encircles a
boy's head. These angelitos are the lucky ones, their dead bodies
lovingly tended, their souls exalted. Won't you join me, dear
reader, in soliciting Heaven's entry for the unlucky boys and girls
massacred alongside their parents in remote villages all over El
Salvador, who while no longer in possession of their bodies—
having fattened maggots long ago—are nonetheless still in posses-
sion of souls deserving a long-delayed entry into paradise. Help
me intercede for those who still have limbs but whose spirits have
withered from watching others ripped apart by machine guns and
machetes, from watching hope and luck eschew them, and for
those whose meager bodies quiver under mylar blankets in
detention cages at the US/Mexico border, for they have cried
and suffered a thousand times over for no other reason than...

Dead and Alive

We die every day
a little more
just ask
the trees outside
your window
in fact as we gather
a new breath
part of us is already
underground
tucked in graves
among the remains
of our dear someones
who took with them
the piece of us
only they knew
as we retain
the piece of them
only we knew

Presagio

Storms
grab you
and you fight
or you let
yourself be taken
either way
you no longer
are a girl holding
the rainbow
you are
down current
thrashing
behind
your shadow
which stands
over the kitchen sink
eating ripe mangoes

2

Of the New Place

Flareup

When the clock strikes twelve
in the new place it will be you
and you also in the old place

Two dictionaries, two maps
one heart, one you

El Salvador, January 1981

For our suitcase held all that was important. For the perils that
awaited were unknown. For the jaguar prowling mountain streams
is a wild beast. For no one asked me what I needed to drink. For
fear was abundant and bodies rotted at the base of zapote trees.
For we fled one country to another so that we could breathe.
For the new country saw not us but our skins. For we had only a
suitcase to begin. For garments fade and shrink on growing limbs.
For memories lap sandy shores and when angry pummel rock.
For how do you fit your world into a two-paneled box? For years
later I saw the same suitcase on a sidewalk thrown and inside,
instead of El Salvador, was a stack of letters, and they, unlike my
memories, in a gust of wind were blown.

Aquí Estoy

This landscape of woman-born
two moons called ovaries
two suns called breasts
on my tongue grafted meanings
from another's language
choking my vernacular

> *Hay mamá me duele la muela,*
> *porque anoche comí ciruela*

between my eyes an open window

> *No soy de aquí—ni soy de allá—no tengo edad*

sometimes a Word, una palabra
clear and unattached, a chip of bone
makes it through, a chip of song
una canción filling my belly
stretching my lungs
        aquí estoy, aquí estoy
playing lotería
swaying my hips to cumbia
comiendo chilate
y pupusas de chicharrón

Chubasco

She returns
to her birth country
a wife and mother
wearing a skirt
long enough to
hide what is necessary
she hopes
that from somewhere
someone calls out,
"Here! See this?
Isn't this what you're searching for?"
she waits
with an unfurled hand
for the appointed
afternoon chubasco
and because today's rain
carries traces of yesteryear
she wonders whether she
could read the water
in past tense
could she see aslant
in the conditional?
see in the droplets
who and how
the person she now is, was?
observe who she might
have become
had she never left
had she never lost
under her left breast

is a window
come closer
notice the brambles, the wildflowers
and among them roses

Arrested Delight

In the cool breeze of midday sheets your tongue blazed across the ocean of my mouth, your hands traced the fervor of my body. I met each gesture—my tongue eager over yours, my hands donating to paradise in the making. You made a comment about the moons of my teeth, something about their ivory gloss, and like that, whatever song I was in vanished. A perfect Sunday afternoon of glittering sunshine turned into a shallow pond no longer swimmable, strewn with trash and rotten fish. This is the story of how decades ago in El Salvador an unscrupulous dentist convinced my mother to exchange enamel for metal. Under those then tropical clouds, war raged around us, even without an official name. Fear spread profusely and over everything. The teeth in question are not as perfect as they seem, their ivory excavated with avarice by an electric drill and replaced by silver fillings. Dental care is expensive in the U.S. the dentist warned, better to take care of future cavities now than to suffer regret. Terror quickly spoiled my mother's face, and the dentist in her starched white coat went in for the kill. What I am trying to say is that war makes you stand outside in the cold when moments before you were luscious inside a dream. Out in the cold you look, mouth ajar, through the tempered glass of a storefront window where candy beckons and an electric train choo choos along over sultry dales and satin sheets, cresting, delivering its passengers satisfactorily to their destinations.

Golden

Ah, how my days hiccup like rain over cobblestone streets.
How what costs you also gains interest. How nothing, not any
thing I can do, can change the events that brought me here. Not
that I would change any of it. Not that the night can be golden,
but because of it.

Wake

Not for what was left behind
nor for what I wish to come
lo que(s)erá será
but for the tight, narrow
abyss between the two

I live at a wake
the lilies on my desk know this
petals paper thin, crumpled
they breathe simultaneous
beauty and decay

outside rain burrows deep
inside the earth
my grief works
the same way
tunnels dug each day

alongside
cardiovascular highways
digestive tracts
lymphatic paths
alongside breath

I remain split
and folks with eagle eyes
and those with doe eyes
offer hands, skin
as a way of unearthing a truth

Cloven Moon

The officer in charge of processing my family's entrance to the
U.S. stated that from that moment on my name was to be Claudia
Castro. The passport says her name is Claudia Castro Luna, my
mother objected. Here we use one last name, said the officer, and
closed the matter with the gavel of his voice. Your moon got taken
away from you, said my friend when I recounted the story. But
when the officer eclipsed the Luna of my name the sensation was
more like having a limb chopped off. For years I walked like that,
cloven, until pen in hand, I began to weave into blank pages
tamales de elote, scent of yerbabuena, spells of flor de muerto,
the riot of a Tuesday market in Ahuachapán, the Nahuatl sageness
of my abuela. I did not know then that weaving like this, warp of
memory, weft of daring, had the power to sew back the name
chopped off at an INS center on a January morning in 1981. All
I know is that one day I walked into a Social Security office, took a
number, and waited my turn to expand the canon of last names
in this country. I pilgrimaged the department of motor vehicles,
registrars' offices, bank-teller windows, and once La Luna hung
again in the firmament of my name, its light spilled beneath my
skin and filtered back into the world from the open mouths of
a million pores.

Farmers Market

I go early to hear the citrus tales of pomelos and satsumas in January, discuss the snap with favas in May, have a word with a merchant without saying anything, hold a coin bag in one hand and with the other chat with an unsuspecting tomato. Market speak is the language of being a girl walking with my mother down narrow lanes in the mercado, sweat streaming brow, impatient dogs weaving between legs, stealthy robbers articulating sneak, sellers shouting incantations to buy this cure-all remedy and for a bargain, una mano—all the fruit that can fit in the palm of your hand. At every turn my local farmers market betrays the one I long for. The mercado I search lives dormant, a tiny seed, rhyming festive, and mom inside my heart.

Less and Less

In the United States, English filled our world the way a cotton ball inside a narrow glass absorbs water. By-and-by some of the Spanish words inside us frayed, while others curled up at the edges. We walked every day across a field and every step toward the center yielded a slip in reverse. Como olas perdidas, su van y ven.

Epicurean Matters

International and East 14th, Tacos Mi Rancho. International and
22nd, Tacos Sinaloa. International and 24th, Tacos Mi Gloria.
International Boulevard asphalt corrido of carnitas and pupusas
de chicharrón. ICE cuotas and remitance receipts. International
and 54th, Tacos Los Amigos. Boa de carne asada. Boca de lengua
frita. Census projections. Future vote tally. And heart, corazón
de rábano, red and crunchy and pulsing with the energy of all
of Guadalupe's children who are many, muchos, son muchos,
muchos somos. International and 80th, Flor de Jalisco. On each
corner, a four-wheeled sentinel guarding the memory of home.
Stand in line, home comes wrapped up, calientito, inside a tor-
tilla. International and 90th, Tacos Union. And though warm,
the bitter seeps in.

Urban Renewal

To my right, decaying Queen Anne Victorians: unkept gardens, ornate entryways, wooden shingles, rich spindle work. Past grandeur fermented with neglect. To my left, thorny nopales nodding to bitter melon, sugarcane stalks yakking with chayote vines, corn checking in with low growing squash. A new celluloid code growing on side yards, in driveways, in metal containers, among and through rambling roses and bearded irises of some-one's romantic yore. Parked on streets, patched up cars. On porches, incense burning, oranges in red bowls, altars unforgetting what in other countries was left behind. The library brochure calls this place the 10th Avenue Historic District. The plants say other-wise. They say, this is what history in the making looks like. Not the crumbling of what was, but what is in the act of becoming.

A Note from the Eastern Front

The boulevard stretches long, long and flat, a taut fraying cord.
Today the sun banishes all shadows at noon. Concrete and burrito
wrappers melt in the heat with plastic calling cards, not enough
money left on them for calls to Tsenzuntepeque, Quezaltenango,
and other towns down south where mothers, daughters, wives,
aunts yearn and haunt the dreams of silenced someones walking
city streets. Walls. Sidewalks vibrate, shout, string words, chords,
audible and visible, a song. A woman pushes a baby in a stroller
with roof to protect from sun's darts, a small girl in uniform
following close behind. Popsicle in hand, she licks lickety-lick—
the lime green slithering to her wrists, lickety-lick—passing the
Arab merchant-owner of the Mexican mercado standing next
to crates bent with fruit. Inside nopales and limes wait under
fluorescent blue and cilantro sings to tomatoes a salsa song.
Somewhere far away a mild sun chases a light rain, forms a sweet
rainbow arched and splendid, stretching as far as the eye can see.
Here, life in its negative space, as far, as far as the eye can see.

Guanaco Tales

A man, like the one I am, steps out of a bus, dressed in black for
his restaurant job, a faded backpack thrown over his shoulder.
A man, like the one I am, speaks into a phone, palabras trailing
behind him like perfume from the billowy blonde clutching the
fancy leather bag. A man walks, eyes affixed to over there, a place
of never-ending wars where butterflies mingle with downpours of
suffering. His words intersect the warm smell of brioche issuing
from the French bakery. I walk, the man I am, while others gawk
at storefront windows searching for what they don't know they
want. Milk, maybe, for the soft mouths of their desires. At the
tiny restaurant the wait is thirty minutes for a table; at the nearby
coffee shop a latte comes with a dose of attitude. Money! How
it glows on cheeks, how it makes wrists sparkle. How loneliness
floats in open gutters. A man, like the one I am, walks and talks
of money for walls and a roof for over there, for paper and pencils,
para leche y miel.

What Work Is

Ramón crouches under shadow sliver cast by the lamppost at
64thand International. He stares ahead, eyes flickering like votive
candle wicks in midday yellow stupor. I call him Ramón though I
don't really know his name—Julio, Juan, Jesus, Ramón—it could be
any of them, none of them, all of them. My father, my brother, my
uncle, my cousin, me. Groups of Ramóns stand at select corners
fishing for work, stand in puddles of bitter and sweet, and in their
hearts mockingbirds sing siesta songs.

Trigger Me a Memory

The word appeared on the corner of West and Sycamore

PAEBAK   GATE   GUAZAPA   GRIEF

A code word like many others sprayed on city walls

GONE   LKA 50   RICH   ONE

A word to cut time, shred it, like shrapnel on skin

CABE   CEKS   GATS   RONS

Three syllables pinch me. Throb in me. Drag me whole

SECRETS   CHILDREN   LOST   BOYS

Guazapa/volcano, Guazapa/civil war, Guazapa/long ago

GIFT GIVER   GUAZAPA   HOSSANA

Guazapa screams at me from the roll-up door of a car repair shop

Held

My neighbor came by to offer me flowers from her garden. She'd
heard about the shootout, of the bullets that shattered our living
room windows, of the gouged gate. We sat in the kitchen. I told
her about standing in front of the house when the figure of a man
dislodged a squall of bullets across my lawn. I told her how A's
two-year-old frame felt against my chest, the baby inside me kick-
ing. My mouth made words. My heart raced. I was in my other
country, crouching from rogue bullets and approaching helicopter
blades, the acrid smell of burnt rubber mixed with panic. Back
then the curtain lifted every day to the precipice of disappeared
family members and friends. We lived on a patch of greyscale.
In the greyness of things, we dreamed, went to school, prayed,
worked. Afternoons my cousin Sofía played the piano. Across the
street in Cecilia's kitchen fresh tortillas awaited the mouths to
which they belonged. Light was light, and sometimes snappy,
like a lemon drop.

Noticias

Each morning news of the dead. Today a headline says homicides are up and a weary community mourns. Most times articles list the names of the departed. This morning the headline reads simply, Man Shot. Somewhere, someone tastes the bitterness, mourns the gait of his step, the sound of his voice, his funny bone. The truth is today's news smells like old news. Like the nameless dead that appeared across El Salvador in the days of the war—broken up, tortured, and left in ditches for birds' beaks. The truth is, in El Salvador, the dead are still showing up mauled and nameless. The truth is, it happens here too. The truth is, they are dead, and we are not. The truth is, we pilfer them, the dead. We leech them for purpose and sharpen pride against their bones. They alone can tell where we are going, and they always know what the piñata holds.

Civitas

A mass shooting on the 300 block of Broadway. The encounter left four wounded and two dead to cap a crime-riddled weekend. Last week, a bullet intended for a young father found instead the infant son he cradled in his arms. My own children came home from school with a special note from the principal explaining that a beloved teacher was one of the dead. The children were told directly that he was shot and died. The school's blue ribbon did not protect him. Good rankings and excellent test scores will not bring him back. Dead is dead. War is war. Diligent, Death escorts all children away from their gardens. At school, children were told no one knows who killed him. But I know who. It is not that hard. Things add up. On our feet, rain. In our pockets, tired refrains. In our hands, stains. And at the ballot box, flames.

Altars on the Streets

Love gestures in no way organized
by a museum or mandated by city decree

we see them often
hugging corner lampposts, pavement bursting
boils of the urban sickness lurking beneath

a mural altar remembering a youth killed
a poster altar at the entrance of a school
each new altar a call—and no suitable response

O wounded city
eye patch worn and heavy heart
stubborn and stumbling over rabid grass

altars at the back of nail shops
altars drawn on taco trucks
altars, too many, soundless on a map

Lotería de los Pobres y Valientes

El Pájaro

Not everybody
makes it up the hill to view
the city's sunset shimmer

when food is scarce, work hours few
park trails fare worse than church pews

El Árbol

Cake crumbs, paper cups
toasts of yesterday's party
rise with the heat

cheers hang still like streamers
from gnarled oak branches

La Mano

Palm reader's jackpot
next to fried chicken spot
some dreams float, others sink

for dollar store find ten dimes
for minimum wage more hard times

El Corazón

Wires   chain   link   fence
blackboard   blacktop   slide   and   learn
"Say no to drugs!" "Stay in school!"

hollow refrains when 'cross from school
mortuary stares, giving youngsters nightmares

La Sirena

Sheila is, be, dead
love leaps from corner wall
torn from light and papa's arms

from dawn to dawn, ill grave
one   forever   sorry   Hell

La Corona

Cedros y ceibas,
tamarindos y aguacates,
our trees! Heart of sky tussling

their green crowns. Dear relatives
we also must leave behind

El Sol

Is all good, peachy
cobbler, sweet potato pie

peace   schools   bread   justice

Panther's urgent vision
more than ever Hallelujah

La Rosa

Las fronteras no existen
preguntale a la Virgen
de Guadalupe

quien derrama bendiciones
sin pedir pasaporte

Monseñor Romero

Today is Día de los Muertos. I took the children to visit Father
Bill. As usual we shared chocolate and pan de muerto. We poured
a lot of chocolate on his piece of bread, and the ground around
his grave swallowed greedily. We could have poured a river. When
Father Bill died, each tear like no other, a river. I cried for each
sister and brother, for the ones who were children and for the
ones who were grown. I cried for me. I cried for you. I cried for
my children, for things they know nothing about. War leaves no
time for grieving. My right to mourn came with Father Bill's fall.
At first glance the U.S. and El Salvador have nothing in common.
Then time revealed the violence of poverty, the violence of drugs,
the violence of guns, and like Monseñor said, the violence of love.

Alchemist

I pick up my abuela's hands
cold and indifferent
hold them between mine
the bones of her fingers
mountains and valleys
under translucent skin

My grandmother's hands
never held mine with
the tenderness I offer hers now
they belonged to her work
her fingers, birds' wings
peeling, chopping, stirring,
tying, wrapping, kneading
she made candies for a living
topped with colored sugars
dressed in coconut flakes

In my childhood days
my abuela's hands were
plump, and smooth and jolly
fingers sporting rings
—the one with the red stone my favorite—
fingers singing life

The rings are gone now
they slipped away
like her memories
of people and things

she once loved
I cradle her hands
birds' wings closing
in this dark adobe house

Luminescence

Pith of heart strings, molar crowns, steel hips. You think your
weight, height, girth make you you. There is truth to that. Body ir-
reducible. Body of proteins and cells. Body of cancer, of stomach
aches. Then there is the body of you swirling down the drain in
the shower stall each morning, the brittleness of your moods, the
longing wedged under your fingernails. You never know. Mysteries
brew and at times in darkness. Under marine rocks squids gestate
ink and locked inside hard shells pearls grow their luminescence.

Thirteen Ways of Looking at a Pupusa

AFTER WALLACE STEVENS' "THIRTEEN WAYS
OF LOOKING AT A BLACKBIRD"

I
Among the photographs in the Sunday paper
of a weekend in Boston
the one right below Paul Revere's statue
the one of a white plate with two pupusas

II
I am certain
birds fly, and
pupusas breed
pleasure

III
Once in the town of Coatepeque
I saw a woman
on a quiet street corner
setting up a pupusa stall
a car went by
dust from the unpaved road
gained height, whirled
it was December
along a white-washed adobe wall
slender and tall, poinsettias burst
scarlet and rich
in the late evening sun

IV
My aunt makes pupusas for a living
she labors over a hot comal
gun shrapnel
from the civil war years
encrusted in the flesh of her strong legs

V
Tarde o temprano
sooner or later
speak of Salvadorans
speak of pupusas

VI
Can anyone deny
the U.S. funding
of the Salvadoran military
during the civil war?

VII
Thousands fled
toward peace
to places where the war
raged only in their heads

VIII
Pupusas are

pupusas have
within their curved boundary
a resistance recipe

IX
O thickheaded members of Congress
debating immigration reform
don't you see the various conquerings
at your feet?
pupusas among them
winning stomachs everywhere
even named "seductive Salvadorans"
in a newspaper culinary review

X
I know of divided allegiances
to country, to language, to history
then I also know
stories need to be told

XI
The red star-spangled banner unfurls
and pupusa signs sprout everywhere

XII
Women birth pupusas
between the palms of wet hands
the maker's lifelines
imprinting the masa
her story—a thousand times told

XIII
We eat war

Each time
a pupusa is made
war sloughs off
undetected and unmeasured
residues
unstable atoms, half-lives

3
Sometimes You Are
Permitted a Return

Pura Vida

Mangos, naranjas,
guayabas, maracas,
ritmo, sabor, sweet nectar

piña para la niña!
jocote para el cipote!

Ask the Bees

On my last trip to El Salvador spiraling down a remote mountain
highway, I spotted a woman and her child sitting on the side
of the road. A sun-bleached umbrella cast shade on her and on
a table stacked with unlabeled glass vessels filled with honey.
Behind her, a steep gorge, ravishing emerald wound, hummed a
tune that told of the beginning of things. The honey came from
there, she said, pointing at the jungle below. Mystery of forest.
Mystery of honey. Necessity of survival. This mother making a
living from the industriousness of hirsute insect faeries harvesting
nectar and iridescent powder from wildflowers, making beauty
edible. The honey emanated a neon glow bright and potent, as if
alive. The force of the gorge, the song of the torogoz, the roar
of the jaguar, the gloss of the leaves, the soil. Volcanic ash hung
suspended inside each container. For us to remember this brilliant
day, I said to Papá handing him a jar. This day when we stood arm
in arm and talked about the war, what it took from all of us, a day
when I asked him to name every tree, every flower we came across
and he did. He named them all, a gesture that said, we are from
here, from this forsaken place where we know the names of things.
On my return, at the Dallas airport, a customs officer confiscated
my jar. Later, in a café waiting for my flight to Seattle, I felt my
cheeks wet, my tears like a meandering rivulet through the lush
terrain that sustained the bees that made the honey that helped
the woman help herself. In the airport's sterile setting I consid-
ered the honey of things. How much time would have to pass
before I'd walk next to my papá once more? How is it that we over-
look what is important? Value the wrong things? What would they
say about the meaning of grief if I asked them, the bees, who turn
sun's fire into edible gem? Magicians and scientists at once, they
have for millennia healed us, nourished us, pollinated this blue

sphere we call home. Those ancient alchemists hunting for the truth and power to transmute base metals into gold searched in vain. Bees have known the secret all along, transforming with exquisite care, which is also love, yellow dust into liquid gold.

Day Stamp

The mango tree

is no longer

but I am

and how lucky

to return

and stand

where it cast

its grace

its shade

over my childhood

all those years ago

Bruja

Back then my classmates called me Chiqui, short for chiquita. By
teacher's orders, I was the one at the front of the line. Chiqui like
a carrot seed. Like an orange pip. Like an acorn. Like possibility.
The word seed may be traced to the Gothic manasēths, mankind,
the world. Chiqui may be traced to the fourth grade at Escuela
Urbana Mixta Madre de El Salvador. Behind the school was a
mountain, plush green, birthing waterfalls. Sihuatehuacán, it was
called. Sihuatl from the Nahuatl, woman. Huacan, a place name.
Some say Sihuatehuacán translates to City of Sorceresses. Sihuatl
making blood each month. Sihuatl madre de todas, water of
waters, an eye for an eye, love for love.

Milpa

Milpa tierna
bajo mirada aguda
de volcanes azules
tallo fuerte
flor de seda
granos de vida
y semilla tenaz
que encontró
campo fértil
dentro de mi

//

Tender green milpas
under blue volcanoes
silken maize tassels
kernels of life
and the hardy seed
that found fertile soil
in me

Sometimes You Are Permitted a Return

Chalice of sunshine my childhood home
adobe walls for the imagination

Roof of memory by way of longing.
When after thirty years I returned to it

I stared past guilt and sadness at the armature
the structure upon which I am built

There on the tile floor, rubble of a long-ago-broken
cup and along the veranda, echoes of old laughter

Scent of fig and bitter orange still hanging, midair
like suspended confetti from a happily broken piñata

My abuela's superstitions and remedies sleeping
in the old kitchen, stacked wood ready for the next fire.

The things of this house I did not know I needed
to find my way out of the labyrinth of exile.

Had I known of bitter and cold I would have
stashed ash and flower into my pockets

But we didn't know then how to read
the palms of our hands. We knew only

what we didn't want, which was death. We wanted
future. To open our mouths, taste sugar, make words.

Ensalada

I am here again. Again sitting, reading in the courtyard of the adobe house where I grew up. In its belly button, which is also mine. Its lush garden one long sigh of glistening leaves. Lanceolate and sagittate, orbicular and reniform, each leaf an emerald goddess. Birds sing today of yesterday, and their trilling enchants and enlivens everything. Up above, a limpid sky. I return to this place often. To this place I return. Always to the trees and the leaves, to the red tiled roof, to the doves. I return. I return to it and drink all of it. Heaven and earth, leaf, flower, stone, like a tall glass of chilled pineapple juice. Better yet, a glass of ensalada. Pedacitos de piña, lechuga y mamey. Pedacitos de infancia, de recuerdos locos y a veces tristes también.

Koky's Song

Y volver, volver, volver,
[…]
quiero volver, volver, volver

    — AS SUNG BY VICENTE FERNÁNDEZ

My cousin Koky lived allá, sin papeles, in the United States.
On the years he managed to return to us, he knew he'd risk his
life trying to get back al Norte, but homesickness cleaved him
with her siren song. He made a party of his first day back, visiting
relatives, sharing stories and beers, a silly smile plastered on his
round face, the echo of his joy rumbling inside his generous belly
made fuller with foods he did not taste in his life up north.
When the beers took hold, he blasted Vicente Fernández singing
"Volver" and waited for the sun to rise. I watched him once from
my bedroom window: he sat cross-legged, a gargoyle perched on
the balcony of our house up in the hills of San Salvador, the city
sparkling faintly below like a nest of fireflies. Ay, ay, ay, how Koky
flew between what could have been and what was, how he cried,
how he sang. A man at the edge of dawn. Not an illegal. Not a
wetback. Not a beaner. Not beaten. Not shamed. A man. A man
come home. A man before the rising sun.

Silent Valentine

Consider the heart, its mighty heft
and how in February two-dimensional
representations of it proliferate
think about how inside a bony ribcage
this giant finds room for all the thinking that it does
how within its humming walls
for decades, childish sentiments dwell
and weighty words unuttered hibernate
take for instance my dilemma
how to express to my father my love
—he spoke to me more often with a belt
which is how his mother nursed him
and how she learned from her father in turn—
maybe my father took to force instead of words
as a way to mitigate his pain
but this is conjecture
rationalizing doesn't make the pain go away
when it comes to love, his definition
has always been less word, more action
he has always been there when it counted most
like when he abandoned country and ideals for my safety
or the years he wasted away in menial jobs for my bread
ah, if only he had taught me using different terms
I could kiss his cheek
seal in an envelope
the coveted three words
but the love I feel for my papá
does not collapse flat
inside a greeting card

it flutters and it kicks
bound to bone and silence
searching for its way out
of the maze inside my chest

A Natural Act

I feed my baby daughter
her noon meal
mashed peas and brown rice
she swallows easily
mouth fast open
after each spoonful
plump face and fervent hands

The last time
I saw my grandmother
I fed her like I now feed my daughter
she sat in a room full of shadows
a crucifix above her bed
she was ghastly looking
emaciated limbs and eyes
staring into space

She opened her mouth
anticipating the water
I held in a cup
but the liquid came back
relief rolling down her chin
and all the while
death watched her
the way ocean waits for river
the great mouth of river's end

Perros de Luna

Dogs howl, bark, and growl at the swollen moon. Perros de Luna,
I think, curled up on my dear dead grandmother's bed. Moon
dogs issuing a bark for each of the dead that haunt us. And there
are so many here, so many, headlining newspapers, stamping
hearts, tattooing hands, exhausting tears. There are the dead who
become saints and the ones who don't. Those with no name and
no face. Those who rot and rot and rot in ditches, dismembered
at the foot of mountains, thrown on railroad tracks. The tender
ones whose bodies later bloom as flowers. The ones who cry all
the day long, the ones who shield you, the ones who avenge, the
ones only dogs can see and greet howling at the moon. Yesterday's
funeral procession, the coffin loaded onto the bed of a pick-up
truck, mourners shuffling in pairs behind, hugging the live edge
of a two-lane road, hands empty, heads bowed. A Blue Bird bus
with sunshine tassels above the driver's window and salsa blaring
rumbled alongside. Deep from evergreen vinyl seats and from the
silence of our hearts, each of us onboard gave thanks it was not
us shuffling along or stiff in the coffin. We let our prayers drift
from open windows, from this bus that in another life, in another
country, carried squiggly children, with good teeth and apples in
their pockets, to school.

Meditation on the Color Purple

The last plums of the season dangle at the tips of soft branches swaying to wind's song. Dressed in garnets and ruby pinks, most were swiftly snatched in early summer. Now those remaining hang black-purple enrobed. They remind me of the widows of my child-hood. Women dressed head-to-toe in mourning, flesh dangling from bare arms, their weathered skin as resilient bark, rheumatic hands softened with unguents of coconut oil and honey balm. Wrinkled women, closed shapes. The last time I saw Doña Elvira she held herself up, her gaunt figure pushed against the threshold of her house, her thin arms wrapped around each other. Her husband long dead, one daughter fallen in war, the other exiled far away, and Yolanda, the strong one, wielding will, her worn machete. The last time I saw Doña Elvira she blended with the smudges on the pale wall turned dusk from mud, sweat, poverty, and war. I walked slowly toward her reeling in the thirty years passed in each other's absence, the ridges on her forehead, the channels in her cheeks, the faint light of her eyes more purple than black. Bitter root, the fear in her body. Terror of falling—shriveled and alone.

Minuta

Cold miracle prepared by the local minutero ambling under
the repurposed umbrella serving as a parasol rigged to the side of
his wooden trolley. Chas, chas, chas—the ice shaver gliding over
the frozen tundra of the ice block. A mountain of crisp flakes,
whiter than any host, packed into a paper cone. To finish it off,
tamarindo, por favor. A thick pour of earthy syrup pitched per-
fectly between sour and sweet. Ideal for all the times life is not.

The Way of Peace

They say gang members guard the entrance to the cemetery with
heat in their hands to extract from visitors a fee to mourn—a sort
of morbid pay perview. Gangs may hover the graveyard, but the
dead, the birds, and the trees were there first. Let them come in
through the bleached gate and keep coming, the birds. Let their
trilling, their feathered warbling spill onto the dead. Let Luis, my
cousin killed at the beginning of the war, six days after he turned
twenty-three, let him rejoice in the chirruping, in the cooling
tree shadows swaying above his humble grave. Let Gladys, who
is buried without a marker because the war washed from her
EVERYTHING—her life, even her name—and is listed instead as
addendum to her mother's cross; let it be the birds to call out
her full name. Let those who went venerably into eternal slumber
like my abuela, my great-uncles, my great-grandmother, my great-
grandfather, who all died as people should—from the rasping of
time against lung—let them enjoy this avian gift. Let all the Castros
and the Leyvas, the Sanchezes and the Quijadas, the dead tucked
inside mausoleums and those whose stiff bones rest quietly under
dirt mounds, let them all reap birdsong. Let them rest in peace.
The way things were before, before dollars and coyotes, gangs,
migra, guerra, before ICE, caravans, and walls. The time before
these words orbited the constellation of our Salvadoran speech.

Sol de Noche

Luna chula. Luna cancha. Luna mechuda. Luna mansa. Luna prieta.
O Luna, you who anchors me in your celestial wake, whose
faintest glow narrows passages where sorrows drift and dwell.
Years ago, the girl of me sensed that the coinage of my thoughts
would forever belong to you. You of the cool gaze pierced through
the riddle I was becoming. Corn moon. Brave moon. Siren moon.
Harvest moon. Mama moon. Always moon.

Cipota Bajo La Luna

She appeared from behind one of the parked cars, her smile
defying night's charcoal light. She was lithe and glowing as if
she had plucked and eaten a chunk of moon. She could not have
been more than six years old. Una cipota earning her keep outside
a well-to-do restaurant in San Salvador, counting on mollified
patrons and her startling presence to conciliate them to their
Christian values. Por favor, she said, extending a hand in our
direction. A coin rested at the heart of it. The truth, and she,
showing us the way. Just then another hand encircled mine. She
watched us walk away in our regalia and into the order of things,
her arm at her side, her hand no richer, and my reflection in
the obsidian mirror of her eyes.

Aguacatero

Useful word, aguacatero, derived from the Nahuatl, ahuacacua-huitl, migrating to aguacate in Spanish, arriving at avocado in English. The generous trees flourish everywhere in El Salvador, edging country roads, spilling their laden branches over adobe fences. In Caliche aguacatero means street dogs. The official title being chucho aguacatero—chucho for dog, aguacatero meaning everywhere available, like the overripe fallen fruit they eat to stave off hunger. Aguacateros trot, starve, fuck, birth, and die on the streets. Eyes preternaturally dialed to plea. Tengo hambre: I am hungry, would you feed me? Tengo sed: I am thirsty, would you quench my thirst? Estoy enfermo: I am sick, my stomach, my sockets, my soul ache, would you cure me? I am itchy, would you exterminate the ticks and fleas gnawing my fur down to raw flesh? Aguacatero means of the horde. It signifies lowest common denominator. But aguacateros are also noble, resilient, clever. The word agua runs through them. Blood runs through them, and fire, flame, and red, the desire to live and prosper. Agua-cateros resemble their two-legged compatriots. Aguacatero means plentiful, like the avocado trees lining roads, roads ahead that await us all, roads we must choose from to survive.

Caliche

This verdant valley is not an ocean, though you can easily see
how once it might have been. Leaves retain a saltiness on their
ribs that tells of ancient waters. Flowering tree vines point to
marine singularities of long ago. If this place was no ocean, it was
a volcanic cauldron. No fairy tale princess has worn a carmine lip
more seductive, more consumed with fever than the carnal pulse
of the red bougainvillea spilling over this adobe fence. Sometimes
in the afternoon's languor, a feeling: lassitude from swimming
in a calid ocean, wave after wave rocking body, trace of water on
skin, wave after wave, the seduction of riding, cresting, the
moan of coming. Silk water whispers, encouraging all manner
of unchecked reproductions from cynicism to packs of drooling
street dogs, starving bitches with the far-away eyes and stiff gait.
Life here is cutting teeth under the fire ball in the heavens. People
checking hunger, checking anger, checking desperation, checking
hope, checking creativity, checking love. And if some idiot were
to throw a match, how it would all catch on fire.

As it has done before.

As it has done before.

May God Grant You a Good Day

Roosters crow no matter noon or dawn, call and respond, back and forth across yards. Sometimes a dog answers. The bicyclist making his way up the road announces fresh bread with a red horn mounted on rusty handlebars. He navigates puddles and swerves by stones while his crater-sized wicker basket harbors rolls with oven heat nestled in their cottony hearts. These are the sounds of happiness. The guava tree brushes shadows onto the old adobe wall, and a pair of doves coo to each other— cucurru-cucu, cucurrucucu—velvet songs of nothing rushed. Around the corner, an ancient wooden Santo, for generations held by the same family, dispenses miracles year-round. El Niño Chiquito, the enigma of his face framed by the worn luster of his silver crown, his infant body resigned to beaded satin and taffeta stitched by local women, their hands swollen from washing clothes, from washing corn with lime, from grinding grain into masa that will be tortillas by noon. In and out of needle. Women darning life, the coming and going between. We love you, they tell the virgin. We love you, they tell her son. We love you, they don't tell each other. They don't tell each other. Instead they mean it when they say, Buenos Dias le de Dios.

Lento

My sister and I washed the oblong seeds clear of any remaining
pulp, placed them in bowls with water, and watched the beard-like
strands undulate in soft waves like tresses of an unconcerned mer-
maid. We gave them names: Tina, Sonia, Paquita. Combed their
hair in pointy updos, radial halos, and swept down along their
bodies. Back in the water, doll spell over their fibers loosened
once more. Lento and pianissimo. The sweet lull of nothing days.

Childhood Syntax

Morning's breeze rolls down red roof tiles, tumbles to the very spot where I write these lines and where, as a girl, I shaped mud pies. Water and soil, filling the crescent of my fingernails, drying ashy on my wrists. I played with my sister patting the mud into soda pop lids and all kinds of toy dishes. We placed the pies in rows, like words in a sentence, already attending to the art of composition. Just now a rushing breeze rattles treetops, cajoles a dry rain. Light sprinkles onto my notebook's open pages. Back then I might have thought the light streaks were sparkles for my baking bread.

Rafters

Tonight I lie down on the bed my grandmother once used.
In the room where an eager seed became my sister. In the room
where I wished for toys to appear Christmas morning at the
foot of my bed. In the room where scorpions made love along
tenebrous rafters. In the room where rain told of thunder
demons through ochre tiles of baked earth. In the room where
my grandmother breathed her last. In the room where her aging
daughter falls asleep dreaming of the children she wanted but
did not have. I lie down in the same room where I dreamt of my
communion, and my mother dreamt of leaving, never to return.

Tinta Florida

Quién dice que solo el arcoiris
se encarga de pintar los días?

Vete a Juayua donde las orquídeas
pulsan cual acuarelas vivas

Veras como entre retoños
tus labios estrenan palabras

Respira entonces los colores
de todas nuestras flores

Y busca entre los pétalos
el sol de todos y del jaguar

4
Aquí Nada Más

On Translation

Vida, vida, vida
vida, vida, vida
vida, vida, vida
vida, vida, vida
vida, vida, vida
not walls

Visions of Gladness

I wish my grandmother's ghost
would gladden every day my slumber

Her stardust halo, her luminous face—
by now I know fear both cages and unbinds

Sometimes I hear her laughter
spiraling toward me like a kindly twister

Fall in, she says, become not the rosary
one bead in front of the other—

Girl, woman, wife, mother, widow—
become pomegranate seeds instead

Each jewel bursting forth from her own papery case
whirling in her own blood by her own light charged

She says this, and this is why on my altar, as she taught me
there is rue, incense, light, and water in a cup

Witness

Beto and I, we work well together. This morning we pruned jasmine vines and blades of flax and picked up fallen camellia blossoms, their petals already corrupted with rust. Once I dreamt of an island on which nothing grew save for a single blooming camellia. She had already dropped hundreds of blossoms and still more bud heads opened at the tips of her sybarite branches. And there, the fuchsia flowers were bright and honest and their bluish tint revealed the sky sleeping inside each. Not a drop of sorrow stained their likenesses. Nearby, a group of faceless grieving figures sat in a circle. Light beamed barely inside them, shrouded as they were with night. They were sisters to the flowers, they said, and meant no harm. Beto and I, we are like the inky shapes. His brothers in the cornfield. Helicopters above. The river nearby. Our hands grieve, soil as our witness, and our slain compatriots, now grubs, inside the earth.

Surafel

In the crook of my arm, inadequate words and a basket of fruit.
Earlier in the day, with hands on hips, I had admonished him:
If you can't control yourself, I will have no choice but to call
your dad! Go ahead, came the reply. He's dead. Stunned by the
response, I stumbled on: How can you say that? The small hand
of the friend sitting behind appeared on his shoulder. The gesture
said it all. Jerk of downward pull, sinking ship inside his wide
boy eyes. Surafel is the apple of my eye, his father said to me at
the last parent-teacher conference we had. The priest at mass did
not say it, but resurrection happens, and daily, in poems and
in our hearts.

Ofrenda

This year the altar in my living room has more portraits than last's. Día de los Muertos, a single day of communion with the dead, but really, all days are theirs. Days of the dead. We require proof. An urn with ashes. A plot under a tree. A shroud holding roses. For the dead it is so. Writing corrupts the waxen page. Sound is unlike water. Never can we hold music in our cupped hands. Such is gravity and time.

Assiduously

From a coffee cup's sweet bitterness into cold wind, knowing
that the place you search and yearn for is nowhere—no street
names, no city gate, no degrees nor longitudinal measures to
speak of. A compass can be useless when you are lost. Nowhere
multiplies in your chest, ravenous like yeast. It hurts. The exact
second of your shadow on the pavement. Sometimes your life
is a minute ahead and a few days behind the place you want to
be. Sometimes things align and you want to tear off a piece of
shadow as you would a piece from a loaf of bread. But this place
you search has no replicable terrain, no map. It moves as you
move. A shapeshifter with a tropic of memory, a tropic of fear, a
meridian to decide you can, and an equator to know you choose.

No More Short Yardsticks to Measure My Days

My daughter's soccer team ended the fall season the number
one seed. Coach says they'll be recognized with pomp and
circumstance at the league's banquet. But not one player wants
to go. We have medals already, they say. What's one more
accolade? I put the toothbrush down, startled by the sound of
my inner voice, licking, like I would a stamp, the word accolade.
I made its acquaintance in the tenth grade. It appeared in the
weekly spelling test. New to English then, I collected words like
a squirrel stashes acorns. Knowing each term meant survival.
Those were the early days of trading tropical sun for winter
snow. Somber days of wearing cotton because wool we could
not afford. Days of dreaming of the gangly boy who sat behind
me in geometry class. We had little in common, down to our
smarts. He leaned over to copy my proofs and I let him. On the
page, the luster of an embrace.

Clearest of Nights

How to make up with yourself after each self-breakup? How to cuddle under a broken wing the girl of you? How to explain that deep inside the sea, sister wind tries on her dress? Snails leave their homes when no one is looking, and birds sometimes are afraid to fly. Who is going to tell you about what only you know? Whose fool will tell spider to spin less? It turns out that you can mend the crevices inside yourself without silk threads and silver spoons. It is possible to tell the truth and not burn in Hell, to win wars without shooting a rifle, and without a rifle to write a poem.

Sueños

Stones bloom yellow roses. Frogs shine shoes. A bat swoops
through the open window to nibble the half-eaten horn I had
with a cup of coffee at 3 p.m. Don Salva's oxen pull the cart over
cobblestone streets, and we children run alongside it, grab hold,
jump in, hand our bodies over to the inertia of jaunty childhood
days. In the courtyard: hanging silver threads and a maze of shiny,
earthly constellations, revelry, and proof of late-night benders
between snails and spiders. In an open field, a flag of nowhere
hoisted. In the sky, my abuela laughing with the stars. Summer
wind bending golden grass. Ocean is there with her mouth wide-
open, saying, atrévete! Jump in, dare yourself!

My Father's Garden

Bears no resemblance
to the orderly paradises found
in glossy magazines
there are no tidy borders to admire
no coordinating color palettes
here the eye is overtaken
by a mass of unapologetic green
olive green, forest green
lemon green, green green

And speckled among the verdure
calling attention to their resplendent selves
are flowers in many hues and shapes
the mallows, my father's favorites
offer blooms as big as birds' nests
petals glisten in midday sun
stretch wide and far
there is little modesty in their display

There is no coyness in this garden
only abundance and overflow
zinnias grow by the dozen
roses burst yellow, salmon, red
bougainvilleas, trumpet flowers
a pulsing profusion
planted all with trembling hands

Twenty exile years
is a long time to contemplate
each new leaf

a coming to terms with lost ideals
each new flower
a testament to fallen friends
each new seedling
a last salute to persecutions of the heart
my father's garden a nascent Eden
a rooting back to his native land

Curcubita Maxima

To be split open with the force of a dull machete, a kind of
coconut fate. To be thirsty walking up a dirt road, hearing
running water through a horsetail thicket but not to see it. That—
of being from here and from there—is a loneliness. From one
bank of the river, an opportunity, a growing pumpkin. From the
other, orange flesh smeared against a porch on Halloween night.
Take me, eye that sees everything, take me through the thicket to
the bend in the river, to the milpa, to mother corn, to the one
Curcubita Maxima that holds my milk teeth and backbone.

Gravity

My body writes its weight into the soft, wet clay, and the page lets me. There is pain here. And dreams. Broken wings. Addictions. Hosannas. Friendships. There are people who look into your eyes. And you into theirs. Plenitude is an arrival. An arrival after a death. I need you. You need me. We need each other. Makes me want to hold on. Hold on to spent blooms and fallen feathers, to aprons and needlework, to wild turkeys, sunsets, warm showers, tendons, hard cocks, and new dawns.

On Citizenship

I want full citizenship
when I die
none of this
you are legal
only when convenient
when cheap labor is wanted
when votes are sought
In Death's camp
there is no Temporary Protected Status
DACA, J-1, or H-2 visas
there are no second chances
short sentences, pardons
no permit renewals
no political expiations
No. Dead is dead
empty days, empty nights
to roam, laugh, spit, love, hate
As hoary ghost
I'll finally own
the full spectrum of me
bitch and saint
rose and stench
I'll make myself
visible and invisible
whenever I want
be mean, or tender
as mother to newborn tender
Ah, when I am dead as dead
boneless, toothless, wordless
wandering somber valleys

among drafts of shadows
when my pride is ground to nothing
and my cry lodges in a mockingbird's throat
what mother of love will I then be!
Better in death to inhabit all of me
than half dead living, living afraid of living
Yes, I want full rights for the ghost of me!
Not just a temporary worker's permit
It shouldn't be that hard
for in life I've never seen
anyone queuing up for the privilege
of crossing to the other side

Mítico // Mythic

Un país con fronteras de pan
Un país donde se camine sin miedo
Un país de leyes con sabor a leche
Un país de muros transparentes color cielo
Un país donde la esperanza no sea ficción
Un país donde el hambre estreche
Un país donde niños no se pudran en prisiones
Un país donde no hay bandera que defender
Un país donde la moneda el calibre de tu corazón es
Un país donde se cambie guerra por algarabía
Un país donde se cante al empezar el día
De ese país quiero ser!

//

A country with borders of bread
A country where one can walk without fear
A country where laws taste like milk
A country where walls are clear
A country where hope is not fiction
A country where hunger is no affliction
A country where children don't rot in jails
A country with no flag to defend
A country where money plays no part
A country where war is broken apart
A country where people begin the day with song
A country where I want to belong

Leave the Gate Open on Your Way Out

On a quiet street
a bloom-laden rosebush
leans into the sidewalk
its orange flowers
swirl and pulse
buds shoot up
to meet the sun
which in time will ripen
their promises
on the same bush
next to fragrance and splendor
in quiet hush
invalid roses drop
fading petals one by one
At the end of the street
stands a hospital
it houses a morgue
and a maternity ward
my own three children
were born within its walls
To give birth is a revolution
leave the gate open
on your way out
better for the angels and the devil
to come and go
the path to happiness
is by way of pain and sorrow
that is something
my abuela could have said
On the quiet street

many pass by the rosebush
exuberant or crestfallen
the shrub stands
ready to share loss and joy
but only with those
who stop to smell its roses

Acknowledgments

Gratitude to:

Irene and Ramón, my parents, for their love and protection;

Sean, Amalia, Beba, and Lucas who support me every day and in multiple ways;

John Pierce for his editorial support;

Museo Nacional de Antropología Dr. David J. Guzmán, El Salvador (MUNA);

Antonio Bonilla for his amazing mural: Mural del Bicentenario;

Olivia Sánchez C. por su creatividad y empeño;

Fred Ramos for the cover photograph;

Rick Simonson por su amistad y apoyo;

Luis J. Rodriguez and Trini Rodriguez for their investment in community;

La más bella, la más tierna, la más chingona, la Santísima Virgen de Guadalupe.

Poems in this collection have appeared previously in other publications, sometimes in earlier versions and under different titles:

"My Father's Garden," *Good News,* 2009

"Wake," *The Womanist,* 2011

"Altars on the Streets," *Riverbabble,* 2013

"Trigger Me a Memory," *Taos International Journal of Poetry and Art,* 2015

"Thirteen Ways of Looking at a Pupusa," *Diálogo,* 2016

"More Daunting Still," *Catalyst Magazine: New Zealand,* 2016

"Tyranny of the Milky Way," *Poetry Northwest,* 2016

"Farmers Market," "Epicurean Matters," "A Note from the Eastern Front," "What Work Is," "Monseñor Romero," "Assiduosly," and "Surafel" in *This City—Chapbook,* Floating Bridge Press, 2016

"Meditation on the Color Purple," *The Wandering Song: Central American Writing in the US,* Leticia Hernández, Ruben Martinez, and Hector Tovar, (Eds.), Tia Chucha Press, 2017.

"Clearest of Nights," *Killing Marías, Two Sylvias,* 2017

"A Natural Act," *King County Poetry on Buses,* 2017

"Sol de Noche," *Poeta Soy: Poesía de Mujeres Salvadoreñas.* Biblioteca Escolar Presidencial: El Salvador, 2018

"On Translation," *Pageboy,* 2019

"Aguacatero," *Kitchen Fires,* Spark Central, 2019

"Ask the Bees," *Texas Review,* 2020